The Swinging Rainbow

Funny and thoughtful, long
and short – this book
contains many kinds of poems:
poems that tell stories and those
that create pictures in the mind;
poems to appeal to a sense of
adventure, and poems about
everyday things.

It is a collection to be read and
enjoyed again and again and there
is something in it for everyone.

The Swinging Rainbow

Poems for the Young
selected by Howard Sergeant

Illustrations by Brian Denyer

 Evans Brothers Limited London

Published by Evans Brothers Limited
Montague House, Russell Square, London, WC1
© Evans Brothers Limited 1969
First published 1969
Reprinted 1969

For Cherrill and Oriel

Set in 12 on 15pt. Imprint
and printed in Great Britain by
Cox & Wyman Ltd, London, Reading and Fakenham
CSD237   35105   6
PB   237   35106   4   PR2339

Contents

Introduction   7
Nursery and Cursory Rhymes   9
Songs and Games   17
Stories in Verse   33
Creatures Wild and Tame   46
Christmas and the New Year   70
Landscapes and Seasons   76
Types and Conditions of Man   90
Battles Lost and Won   100
Man's Endless Quest   110
Night-time and Dreams   117
Index of Authors   125
Index of First Lines   126

Acknowledgements

For permission to use copyright material the editor and publishers are indebted to the following:

Angus & Robertson Ltd. for 'Legend' from *Five Senses* by Judith Wright; Mrs. George Bambridge and Macmillan & Co. Ltd. for 'The Way Through the Woods' from *Rewards and Fairies* by Rudyard Kipling; Miss D. E. Collins and J. M. Dent & Sons, Ltd. for 'The Donkey' from *The Wild Knight and Other Poems* by G. K. Chesterton; The Literary Trustees of Walter de la Mare and the Society of Authors as their representative for 'The Storm' by Walter de la Mare; the author for 'The Giraffe' by Geoffrey Dearmer; Faber & Faber Ltd. for 'Macavity the Mystery Cat' from *Old Possum's Book of Practical Cats* by T. S. Eliot, and 'Dunkirk 1940' from *Tonypandy* by Idris Davies; the author for 'Rocket to the Moon' by Douglas Gibson, and 'Looking at Stars' by Phoebe Hesketh; Sidgwick & Jackson Ltd. for 'Ducks' from *Ducks and Other Poems* by F. W. Harvey; the Society of Authors as the literary representative of the Estate of John Masefield for the extract from 'Reynard the Fox'; the author for 'Sampler' by Howard Sergeant.

Introduction

In this collection you will find poems to match every mood, and, almost demanding their rightful place, a few nursery rhymes and traditional songs.

Nursery rhymes might be described as the beginnings of poetry. We learn them readily for the sheer joy of the words and rhythms, without knowing, or even caring, that many of them had a much deeper meaning for the time in which they first appeared. Little Jack Horner, Jack and Jill, the King of Spain's daughter, the Frog who would a-Wooing Go, Georgie-Porgie who kissed the girls, and lots of others, apart from being quaint characters, all had real historical meaning at one time or another and had to be disguised as nursery rhymes. In some cases the poet might have been in danger of losing his head if the rulers at the time had known about whom he was actually writing.

Did you know, for instance, that 'Mary, Mary, Quite Contrary' may well have been Mary, Queen of Scots, the 'pretty maids' her ladies-in-waiting, and the 'cockleshells' decorations on a dress given to her by a French prince? Or that the 'Old Woman who lived in a Shoe' and had so many children, has been identified as Queen Caroline, wife of George II, who had a large family of eight children? Or that the king 'counting out his money' in 'Sing a Song of Sixpence' was no other than the famous

Henry VIII who closed down the monasteries (taking some of their treasures) in the sixteenth century; the queen in the parlour, his wife Katherine; and the maid who had her nose snapped off in the garden, Anne Boleyn?

I have also included some of our fine traditional songs because they happen also to be good poems, too. That is not surprising when we remember that music and poetry share the same origins in song, on the one hand, and in dancing, on the other. The earliest poetry of all *was* song.

I have always believed that, whatever the age or taste of the reader, poetry was meant to be enjoyed; and in compiling this collection I have had this particularly in mind. I might easily have called the book 'Poems for Enjoyment', for the best poets have always been concerned with life in all its astonishing variety – the little everyday things which fill up most of our days as well as the big events which interest us as we grow older. I hope that the poems you will find here bring you enjoyment and that, for you, 'the swinging rainbow' will always shine 'as brightly as the sun', as it did for the blacksmith's boy in the poem *Legend* by one of Australia's finest poets, Judith Wright:

> He went home as easy as could be
> with the swinging rainbow on his shoulder.

HOWARD SERGEANT

Nursery and Cursory Rhymes

Monday's Child   10
Little Jack Horner   10
Mary, Mary, Quite Contrary   11
Eaper Weaper – *London Street Game*   11
A Little Cock Sparrow   11
Sing a Song of Sixpence   12
The Man Who Wasn't There   12
There Was a Crooked Man   13
There Was an Old Woman Who Lived in a
    Shoe   13
The Grand Old Duke of York   14
Don't Care   14
Weather   15
Answer to a Child's Question *by Samuel
    Taylor Coleridge*   15
The Vowels by *Jonathan Swift*   16
How Many Miles to Babylon?   16

Monday's Child

Monday's child is fair of face,
Tuesday's child is full of grace,
Wednesday's child is full of woe,
Thursday's child has far to go,
Friday's child is loving and giving,
Saturday's child works hard for his living,
And the child that is born on the Sabbath day
Is bonny and blithe, and good and gay.

Little Jack Horner

Little Jack Horner
Sat in a corner,
Eating a Christmas pie;
He put in his thumb
And pulled out a plum,
And said, What a good boy am I!

Mary, Mary, Quite Contrary

Mary, Mary, quite contrary,
    How does your garden grow?
With silver bells and cockle shells,
    And pretty maids all in a row.

Eaper Weaper

Eaper Weaper, chimbley-sweeper,
Had a wife but couldn't keep her,
Had annovver, didn't love her,
Up the chimbley he did shove her.

LONDON STREET GAME

A Little Cock Sparrow

A little cock sparrow sat on a tree,
Looking as happy as happy could be,
Till a boy came by with his bow and arrow:
Says he, 'I'll shoot that little cock sparrow.

His body will make a nice little stew,
And perhaps there'll be some for a little pie too.'
Says the little cock sparrow, 'I'll be shot if I
    stay.'
So he flapped his wings and flew away!

Sing a Song of Sixpence

Sing a song of sixpence,
  A pocket full of rye;
Four and twenty blackbirds,
  Baked in a pie.

When the pie was opened,
  The birds began to sing;
Was not that a dainty dish
  To set before the king?

The king was in his counting-house,
  Counting out his money;
The queen was in the parlour,
  Eating bread and honey.

The maid was in the garden,
  Hanging out the clothes,
There came a little blackbird,
  And snapped off her nose.

The Man Who Wasn't There

As I was going up the stair
I met a man who wasn't there.
He wasn't there again today –
Oh, how I wish he'd go away.

There Was a Crooked Man

There was a crooked man, and
  He walked a crooked mile,
He found a crooked sixpence
  Against a crooked stile;
He bought a crooked cat, which
  Caught a crooked mouse,
And they all lived together in
  A little crooked house.

There Was an Old Woman
Who Lived in a Shoe

There was an old woman who lived in a shoe,
She had so many children she didn't know what
  to do;
She gave them some broth without any bread;
She whipped them all soundly and put them to
  bed.

The Grand Old Duke of York

O, the grand old Duke of York,
   He had ten thousand men;
He marched them up to the top of the hill
   And he marched them down again!

When they were up, they were up,
   When they were down, they were down,
And when they were only half-way up,
   They were neither up nor down.

Don't-Care

Don't-Care – he didn't care,
   Don't-Care was wild:
Don't-Care stole plum and pear
   Like any beggar's child.

Don't-Care was made to care,
   Don't-Care was hung;
Don't-Care was put in a pot
   And stewed till he was done.

Weather

Whether the weather be fine,
   Or whether the weather be not,
Whether the weather be cold,
   Or whether the weather be hot,
We'll weather the weather,
   Whatever the weather,
Whether we like it or not.

Answer to a Child's Question

Do you ask what the birds say? The sparrow and
   the dove,
The linnet, and thrush say, 'I love, and I love!'
In the winter they're silent, the wind is so
   strong;
What it says I don't know, but it sings a loud
   song.
But green leaves, and blossoms, and sunny
   warm weather,
And singing and loving – all come back together.
But the lark is so brimful of gladness and love,
The green fields below him, the blue sky above,
That he sings, and he sings, and for ever sings
   he,
'I love my Love, and my Love loves me.'

SAMUEL TAYLOR COLERIDGE

The Vowels

We are very little creatures,
All of different voice and features;
One of us in glAss is set,
One of us you'll find in jEt,
T'other you may see in tIn,
And the fourth a bOx within,
If the fifth you would pursue,
It can never fly from yoU.

JONATHAN SWIFT

How Many Miles to Babylon?

How many miles to Babylon?
   Three-score miles and ten.
Can I get there by candle-light?
   Yes, and back again.
If your heels are nimble and light,
   You may get there by candle-light.

Songs and Games

Old Roger – *Street Game*   18

Fire Down Below – *Sea Shanty*   19

Down in the Meadow – *Northampton Street Game*   20

Guy Fawkes – *Game*   21

John Barleycorn – *Folk Song*   22

London Bridge – *Traditional Song*   24

A Fox Jumped Up One Winter's Night – *Traditional Song*   26

One More River – *Folk Song*   28

Soldier, Soldier – *Folk Song*   31

Song *by William Shakespeare*   32

Old Roger

Old Roger is dead and gone to his grave,
H'm, ha! gone to his grave.

They planted an apple tree over his head,
H'm, ha! over his head.

The apples grew ripe and ready to drop,
H'm ha! ready to drop.

There came a high wind and blew them all off,
H'm, ha! blew them all off.

There came an old woman to pick them all up.
H'm ha! pick them all up.

Old Roger got up and gave her a knock,
H'm, ha! gave her a knock,

Which made the old woman go hipperty-hop,
H'm, ha! hipperty hop.

STREET GAME

Fire Down Below

Fire in the galley, fire down below,
It's fetch a bucket of water, boys,
There's fire down below.
Fire, fire,
Fire down below,
It's fetch a bucket of water, boys,
There's fire down below.

Fire in the forepeak, fire down below,
It's fetch a bucket of water, boys,
There's fire down below.
Fire, fire,
Fire down below,
It's fetch a bucket of water, boys,
There's fire down below.

Fire in the windlass, fire in the chain,
It's fetch a bucket of water, boys,
And put it out again.
Fire, fire,
Fire down below,
It's fetch a bucket of water, boys,
There's fire down below.

Fire up aloft, and fire down below,
It's fetch a bucket of water, boys,
There's fire down below.
Fire, fire,
Fire down below,
It's fetch a bucket of water, boys,
There's fire down below.

SEA SHANTY

Down in the Meadow

Down in the meadow
Where the green grass grows,
To see Sally Waters
Bloom like a rose:
Sally made a pudding,
She made it so sweet,
And never stuck a knife in
Till Johnny came to eat.
Taste love, taste love,
And don't say nay,

For next Monday morning
Is your wedding day.
He bought her a gown
And a guinea-gold ring,
And a fine cocked hat
To be married in.

NORTHAMPTON STREET GAME

Guy Fawkes

Guy Fawkes, Guy!
A penny for the Guy!

Please to remember
The fifth of November
  Gunpowder treason and plot;
I see no reason
Why gunpowder treason
  Should ever be forgot.

Guy Fawkes, Guy!
A penny for the Guy!

Guy Fawkes, Guy Fawkes, 'twas his intent
To blow up the King and the Parliament,
But by God's providence him they catch,
With a dark lanthorn, lighting a brimstone
  match.
Holler boys, holler boys, make your voices ring
Holler boys, holler boys, *God save the King!*
  Hip, hip, hooray!

21

John Barleycorn

There came three men from out the West
　　Their victory to try;
And they have taken a solemn oath
　　John Barleycorn should die.

They took a plough and ploughed him in,
　　Laid clods upon his head,
And they have taken a solemn oath
　　John Barleycorn is dead.

So there he lay for a full fortnight,
　　Till the dew from heaven did fall;
John Barleycorn sprang up again,
　　And sore surprised them all.

But when he faced the summer sun,
　　He looked both pale and wan –
For all he had a spiky beard
　　To show he was a man.

But soon came men with sickles sharp
　　And chopped him to the knee.
They rolled and tied him by the waist
　　And served him barbarously.

With forks they stuck him to the heart
   And banged him over stones,
And sent the men with holly clubs
   To batter at his bones.

But Barleycorn has noble blood:
   It lives when it is shed:
It fills the cupboard and the purse
   With gold and meat and bread.

O Barleycorn is the choicest grain
   That e'er was sown on land;
It will do more than any grain
   By the turning of your hand.

FOLK SONG

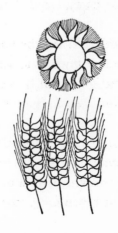

London Bridge

London Bridge is broken down
  Dance o'er my Lady Lee,
London Bridge is broken down,
  With a gay lady.

How shall we build it up again?
  Dance o'er my Lady Lee,
How shall we build it up again?
  With a gay lady.

Build it up with silver and gold,
  Dance o'er my Lady Lee,
Build it up with silver and gold,
  With a gay lady.

Silver and gold will be stole away,
  Dance o'er my Lady Lee,
Silver and gold will be stole away,
  With a gay lady.

Build it up with iron and steel,
  Dance o'er my Lady Lee,
Build it up with iron and steel,
  With a gay lady.

Iron and steel will bend and bow,
Dance o'er my Lady Lee,
Iron and steel will bend and bow,
With a gay lady.

Build it up with wood and clay,
Dance o'er my Lady Lee,
Build it up with wood and clay,
With a gay lady.

Wood and clay will wash away,
Dance o'er my Lady Lee,
Wood and clay will wash away,
With a gay lady.

Build it up with stone so strong,
Dance o'er my Lady Lee.
Huzza! 'twill last for ages long,
With a gay lady.

TRADITIONAL SONG

A Fox Jumped Up One Winter's Night

A fox jumped up one winter's night,
And he begged the moon to give him light,
For he'd many miles to trot that night
Before he reached his den O!
      Den O! Den O!
For he'd many miles to trot that night
Before he reached his den O!

The first place he came to was a farmer's yard,
Where the ducks and the geese declared it hard
That their nerves should be shaken and their
  rest so marred
By a visit from Mr. Fox O!
      Fox O! Fox O!
That their nerves should be shaken and their
  rest so marred
By a visit from Mr. Fox O!

He took the grey goose by the neck,
And swung him right across his back;
The grey goose cried out, Quack, quack, quack,
With his legs hanging dangling down O!
      Down O! Down O!
The grey goose cried out, Quack, quack, quack,
With his legs hanging dangling down O!

Old Mother Slipper Slopper jumped out of bed,
And out of the window she popped her head:
Oh! John, John, John, the grey goose is gone,
And the fox is off to his den O!
        Den O! Den O!
Oh! John, John, John, the grey goose is gone,
And the fox is off to his den O!

John ran up to the top of the hill,
And blew his whistle loud and shrill;
Said the fox, That is very pretty music; still –
I'd rather be in my den O!
        Den O! Den O!
Said the fox, That is very pretty music; still –
I'd rather be in my den O!

The fox went back to his hungry den,
And his dear little foxes, eight, nine, ten;
Quoth they, good daddy, you must go there
    again,
If you bring such good cheer from the farm O!
        Farm O! Farm O!
Quoth they, good daddy, you must go there
    again,
If you bring such good cheer from the farm O!

The fox and his wife, without any strife,
Said they never ate a better goose in all their life;
They did very well without fork or knife,
And the little ones picked the bones O!
      Bones O! Bones O!
They did very well without fork or knife,
And the little ones picked the bones O!

TRADITIONAL SONG

One More River

Old Noah once built the ark,
There's one more river to cross;
And patched it up with hickory bark,
There's one more river to cross.
One more river, and that's the river of Jordan;
One more river, there's one more river to cross.

He went to work to load his stock,
There's one more river to cross;
He anchored the ark with a great big rock,
There's one more river to cross.
One more river, etc.

The animals went in one by one;
There's one more river to cross;
The elephant chewing a caraway bun,
There's one more river to cross.
One more river, etc.

The animals went in two by two,
There's one more river to cross;
The centipede with the kangeroo,
There's one more river to cross.
One more river, etc.

The animals went in three by three,
There's one more river to cross;
The bear, the flea, and the bumble bee,
There's one more river to cross.
One more river, etc.

The animals went in four by four,
There's one more river to cross;
The camel, he got stuck in the door,
There's one more river to cross.
One more river, etc.

The animals went in five by five,
There's one more river to cross;
Some were tired, more dead than alive,
There's one more river to cross.
One more river, etc.

The animals went in six by six,
There's one more river to cross;
The monkey he was up to his tricks,
There's one more river to cross.
One more river, etc.

The animals went in seven by seven,
There's one more river to cross;
Said the ant to the elephant, who are you
    shoving?
There's one more river to cross.
One more river, etc.

The animals went in eight by eight,
There's one more river to cross;
The worm was early, the bird was late,
There's one more river to cross.
One more river, etc.

The animals went in nine by nine,
There's one more river to cross;
Old Noah shouted: 'Cut that line';
There's one more river to cross.
One more river, etc.

The animals went in ten by ten,
There's one more river to cross;
If you want any more you must sing it again,
There's one more river to cross.

*One more river, and that's the river of Jordan;
One more river, there's one more river to cross.*

FOLK SONG

Soldier, Soldier

'Oh! Soldier, soldier, won't you marry me,
　　With your musket, fife and drum?'
'*Oh no, sweet maid, I cannot marry thee,*
　　For I have no coat to put on.'

So up she went to her grandfather's chest,
And she got him a coat of the very, very best
　　And the soldier put it on!

'Oh! Soldier, soldier, won't you marry me,
　　With your musket, fife and drum?'
'*Oh no, sweet maid, I cannot marry thee,*
　　For I have no hat to put on.'

So up she went to her grandfather's chest,
And she got him a hat of the very, very best
　　And the soldier put it on!

'Oh! Soldier, soldier, won't you marry me,
　　With your musket, fife and drum?'
'*Oh no, sweet maid, I cannot marry thee,*
　　For I have no boots to put on.'

So up she went to her grandfather's chest,
And she got him a pair of the very, very best
　　And the soldier put them on!

'Oh! Soldier, soldier, won't you marry me,
  With your musket, fife and drum?'
'Oh no, sweet maid, I cannot marry thee,
  For I have a wife of my own!'

FOLK SONG

Song

When icicles hang by the wall,
  And Dick the shepherd blows his nail,
And Tom bears logs into the hall,
  And milk comes frozen home in pail;
When blood is nipped, and ways be foul,
Then nightly sings the staring owl.
Tu-whit, tu-who! A merry note!
While greasy Joan doth keel the pot.

When all about the wind doth blow,
  And coughing drowns the parson's saw,
And birds sitting brooding in the snow,
  And Marian's nose looks red and raw,
When roasted crabs hiss in the bowl,
Then nightly sings the staring owl,
Tu-whit, tu-who! A merry note!
While greasy Joan doth keel the pot.

WILLIAM SHAKESPEARE

Stories in Verse

The Jumblies *by Edward Lear* 34
Choosing Their Names *by Thomas Hood* 38
The Fakenham Ghost *by Robert Bloomfield* 39
The Mad Gardener's Song *by Lewis Carroll* 42
The Ant and the Cricket 44

The Jumblies

They went to sea in a Sieve, they did,
   In a Sieve they went to sea:
In spite of all their friends could say,
On a winter's morn, on a stormy day,
   In a Sieve they went to sea!
And when the Sieve turned round and round,
And every one cried, 'You'll all be drowned!'
They called aloud, 'Our Sieve ain't big,
But we don't care a button! we don't care a fig!
   In a Sieve we'll go to sea!'
     Far and few, far and few,
       Are the lands where the Jumblies live;
      Their heads are green, and their hands are
         blue,
      And they went to sea in a Sieve.

They sailed away in a Sieve, they did,
   In a Sieve they sailed so fast,
With only a beautiful pea-green veil
Tied with a riband by way of a sail,
   To a small tobacco-pipe mast;
And every one said, who saw them go,
'O won't they be soon upset, you know!
For the sky is dark, and the voyage is long,
And happen what may, it's extremely wrong
   In a Sieve to sail so fast!'

Far and few, far and few,
    Are the lands where the Jumblies live;
  Their heads are green, and their hands are
        blue,
    And they went to sea in a Sieve.

The water it soon came in, it did,
    The water it soon came in;
So to keep them dry, they wrapped their feet
In a pinky paper all folded neat,
    And they fastened it down with a pin.
And they passed the night in a crockery-jar,
And each of them said, 'How wise we are!
Though the sky be dark, and the voyage be long,
Yet we never can think we were rash or wrong,
    While round in our Sieve we spin!'
      Far and few, far and few,
        Are the lands where the Jumblies live;
      Their heads are green, and their hands are
            blue,
        And they went to sea in a Sieve.

And all night long they sailed away;
    And when the sun went down,
They whistled and warbled a moony song
To the echoing sound of a coppery gong,
    In the shade of the mountains brown.

'O Timballo! How happy we are,
When we live in a Sieve and a crockery-jar,
And all night long in the moonlight pale,
We sail away with a pea-green sail,
  In the shade of the mountains brown!'
    Far and few, far and few,
      Are the lands where the Jumblies live;
      Their heads are green, and their hands are
          blue,
      And they went to sea in a Sieve.

They sailed to the Western Sea, they did,
  To a land all covered with trees,
And they bought an Owl, and a useful Cart,
And pound of Rice, and a Cranberry Tart,
  And a hive of silvery Bees.
And they bought a Pig, and some green
          Jack-daws,
And a lovely Monkey with lollipop paws,
And forty bottles of Ring-Bo-Ree,
  And no end of Stilton Cheese.
    Far and few, far and few,
      Are the lands where the Jumblies live;
      Their heads are green and their hands are
          blue,
      And they went to sea in a Sieve.

And in twenty years they all came back,
   In twenty years or more,
And every one said, 'How tall they've grown!
For they've been to the Lakes, and the Terrible
       Zone,
   And the hills of the Chankly Bore';
And they drank their health, and gave them **a**
       feast
Of dumplings made of beautiful yeast;
And every one said, 'If we only live,
We too will go to sea in a Sieve –
   To the hills of the Chankly Bore!'
     Far and few, far and few,
       Are the lands where the Jumblies live;
      Their heads are green, and their hands are
       blue,
     And they went to sea in a Sieve.

EDWARD LEAR

Choosing Their Names

Our old cat has kittens three –
What do you think their names should be?

One is a tabby with emerald eyes,
And a tail that's long and slender,
And into a temper she quickly flies
    If you ever by chance offend her.
        I think we shall call her this –
        I think we shall call her that –
Now, don't you think that *Pepperpot*
        Is a nice name for a cat?

One is black with a frill of white,
    And her feet are all white fur,
If you stroke her she carries her tail upright
    And quickly begins to purr.
        I think we shall call her this –
        I think we shall call her that –
Now, don't you think that *Sootikin*
        Is a nice name for a cat?

One is a tortoiseshell, yellow and black,
  With plenty of white about him;
If you tease him, at once he sets up his back,
  He's a quarrelsome one, ne'er doubt him.
    I think we shall call him this –
    I think we shall call him that –
Now, don't you think that *Scratchaway*
    Is a nice name for a cat?

Our old cat has kittens three
And I fancy these their names will be:
Pepperpot, Sootikin, Scratchaway – there!
Were ever kittens with these to compare?
And we call the old mother –
    Now, what do you think? –
    Tabitha Longclaws Tiddley Wink.

THOMAS HOOD

The Fakenham Ghost

The lawns were dry in Euston park:
(Here truth inspires my tale),
The lonely footpath, still and dark,
Led over hill and dale.

Benighted was an ancient dame,
And fearful haste she made
To gain the vale of Fakenham,
And hail its willow shade.

Her footsteps knew no idle stops,
But followed faster still;
And echoed to the darksome copse
That whispered on the hill.

Darker it grew, and darker fears
Came o'er her troubled mind;
When now, a short, quick step she hears,
Come patting close behind.

She turned, it stopped; nought could she see
Upon the gloomy plain;
But as she strove the sprite to flee,
She heard the same again.

Now terror seized her quaking frame,
For, where her path was bare,
The trotting ghost kept on the same –
She muttered many a prayer.

Yet once again, amidst her fright,
She tried what sight could do;
When, through the cheating glooms of night,
A *Monster* stood in view.

Regardless of whate'er she felt,
It followed down the plain;
She owned her sins, and down she knelt,
And said her prayers again.

Then on she sped, and hope grew strong,
The white park-gate in view;
Which pushing hard, so long it swung,
That ghost and all passed through!

Loud fell the gate against the post,
Her heart-strings like to crack;
For much she feared the grisly ghost
Would leap upon her back.

Still on – pit-pat – the goblin went,
As it had done before;
Her strength and resolution spent,
She fainted at the door.

Out came her husband, much surprised,
Out came her daughter dear;
Goodnatured souls! all unadvised
Of what they had to fear.

The candle's gleam pierced through the night,
Some short space o'er the green;
And there the little trotting sprite
Distinctly might be seen.

An ass's foal had lost its dam
Within the spacious park;
And, simple as a playful lamb,
Had followed in the dark.

No goblin he; no imp of sin;
No crimes had ever known;
They took the shaggy stranger in,
And reared him as their own.

ROBERT BLOOMFIELD

The Mad Gardener's Song

He thought he saw an Elephant,
   That practised on a fife:
He looked again, and found it was
   A letter from his wife.
'At length I realize,' he said,
   'The bitterness of Life!'

He thought he saw a Buffalo
   Upon the chimney-piece:
He looked again, and found it was
   His Sister's Husband's Niece.
'Unless you leave this house,' he said,
   'I'll send for the police!'

He thought he saw a Rattlesnake
    That questioned him in Greek:
He looked again, and found it was
    The Middle of Next Week.
'The one thing I regret,' he said,
    'Is that it cannot speak!'

He thought he saw a Banker's Clerk
    Descending from a bus:
He looked again, and found it was
    A Hippopotamus:
'If this should stay to dine,' he said,
    'There won't be much for us!'

He thought he saw a Kangaroo
    That worked a coffee-mill:
He looked again, and found it was
    A vegetable-Pill.
'Were I to swallow this,' he said,
    'I should be very ill!'

He thought he saw a Coach-and-Four
    That stood beside his bed:
He looked again, and found it was
    A Bear without a Head.
'Poor thing,' he said, 'poor silly thing!
    It's waiting to be fed!'

                                    LEWIS CARROLL

The Ant and the Cricket

A silly young cricket, accustomed to sing
Through the warm, sunny months of gay
   summer and spring,
Began to complain, when he found that at home
His cupboard was empty and winter was come.
       Not a crumb to be found
       On the snow-covered ground;
       Not a flower could he see,
       Not a leaf on a tree;
'Oh, what will become,' says the cricket, 'of me?'

At last by starvation and famine made bold,
All dripping with wet and all trembling with
   cold,
Away he set off to a miserly ant,
To see if, to keep him alive, he would grant
       Him shelter from rain:
       A mouthful of grain
       He wished only to borrow,
       He'd repay it tomorrow:
If not, he must die of starvation and sorrow.

Says the ant to the cricket, 'I'm your servant
  and friend,
But we ants never borrow, we ants never lend;
But tell me, dear sir, did you lay nothing by
When the weather was warm?' Said the cricket,
  'Not I.

     My heart was so light
     That I sang day and night,
     For all nature looked gay.'
     'You *sang*, sir, you say?
Go then,' said the ant, 'and *dance* winter away!'

Thus ending, he hastily lifted the wicket
And out of the door turned the poor little cricket.

Creatures Wild and Tame

Clock-a-Clay *by John Clare* 47
The Skylark *by Christina Rossetti* 48
Horses *by Christina Rossetti* 48
Macavity the Mystery Cat *by T. S. Eliot* 49
The Owl *by Lord Tennyson* 52
The Donkey *by G. K. Chesterton* 53
The Kangaroo 54
Derby Ram 54
How Doth the Little Crocodile *by Lewis Carroll* 57
Old Man Platypus *by A. B. Paterson* 58
To a Black Greyhound *by Julian Grenfell* 59
The Giraffe *by Geoffrey Dearmer* 60
From Reynard the Fox *by John Masefield* 62
Ducks *by F. W. Harvey* 66

Clock-a-Clay

In the cowslip pips I lie,
Hidden from the buzzing fly,
While green grass beneath me lies,
Pearled with dew like fishes' eyes,
Here I lie, a clock-a-clay,
Waiting for the time o' day.

While grassy forest quakes surprise,
And the wild wind sobs and sighs,
My gold home rocks as like to fall,
On its pillar green and tall;
When the pattering rain drives by
Clock-a-clay keeps warm and dry.

Day by day and night by night,
All the week I hide from sight;
In the cowslip pips I lie,
In rain and dew still warm and dry,
Day and night, and night and day,
Red, black-spotted clock-a-clay.

My home shakes in wind and showers,
Pale green pillar topped with flowers,
Bending at the wild wind's breath,
Till I touch the grass beneath;
Here I live, lone clock-a-clay,
Watching for the time of day.

JOHN CLARE

The Skylark

The earth was green, the sky was blue:
  I saw and heard one sunny morn
A skylark hang between the two,
  A singing speck above the corn;

A stage below, in gay accord
  White butterflies danced on the wing,
And still the singing skylark soared,
  And silent sank and soared to sing.

The cornfield stretched a tender green
  To right and left beside my walks;
I knew he had a nest unseen
  Somewhere among the million stalks.

And as I paused to hear his song,
  While swift the sunny moments slid,
Perhaps his mate sat listening long,
  And listened longer than I did.

CHRISTINA ROSSETTI

Horses

The horses of the sea
  Rear a foaming crest,
But the horses of the land
  Serve us the best.

The horses of the land,
   Munch corn and clover,
While the foaming sea-horses
   Toss and turn over.

CHRISTINA ROSSETTI

Macavity the Mystery Cat

Macavity's a Mystery Cat; he's called the Hidden
   Paw –
For he's the master criminal who can defy the law.
He's the bafflement of Scotland Yard, the Flying
   Squad's despair:
For when they reach the scene of crime –
   Macavity's not there!

Macavity, Macavity, there's no one like Macavity,
He's broken every human law, he breaks the
   law of gravity.
His powers of levitation would make a fakir stare,
And when you reach the scene of crime –
   Macavity's not there!
You may seek him in the basement, you may
   look up in the air –
But I tell you once and once again, *Macavity's
   not there!*

Macavity's a ginger cat, he's very tall and thin;
You would know him if you saw him, for his
   eyes are sunken in.
His brow is deeply lined with thought, his head
   is highly domed;
His coat is dusty from neglect, his whiskers are
   uncombed.
He sways his head from side to side, with
   movements like a snake;
And when you think he's half asleep, he's always
   wide awake.

Macavity, Macavity, there's no one like
   Macavity,
For he's a fiend in feline shape, a monster of
   depravity.
You may meet him in a by-street, you may see
   him in the square –
But when a crime's discovered, then *Macavity's
not there!*

He's outwardly respectable. (They say he cheats
   at cards.)
And his footprints are not found in any file of
   Scotland Yard's.
And when the larder's looted, or the jewel-case
   is rifled,
Or when the milk is missing, or another Peke's
   been stifled,

Or the greenhouse glass is broken, and the
   trellis past repair –
Ay, there's the wonder of the thing! *Macavity's
   not there!*

And when the Foreign Office find a Treaty's
   gone astray,
Or the Admiral's lost some plans and drawings by
   the way,
There may be a scrap of paper in the hall or on
   the stair –
But it's useless to investigate – *Macavity's not
   there!*
And when the loss has been disclosed, the
   Secret service say:
'It *must* have been Macavity!' – but he's a mile
   away.
You'll be sure to find him resting, or a-licking of
   his thumbs,
Or engaged in doing complicated long division
   sums.

Macavity, Macavity, there's no one like Macavity,
There never was a Cat of such deceitfulness and
   suavity.
He always has an alibi, and one or two to spare:
At whatever time the deed took place –
   Macavity wasn't there!

And they say that all the Cats whose wicked
    deeds are widely known
(I might mention Mungojerrie, I might mention
    Griddlebone)
Are nothing more than agents for the Cat who
    all the time
Just controls their operations: the Napoleon of
    Crime!

T. S. ELIOT

The Owl

When cats run home and light is come,
    And dew is cold upon the ground,
And the far-off stream is dumb,
    And the whirring sail goes round,
    And the whirring sail goes round;
        Alone and warming his five wits,
        The white owl in the belfry sits.

When merry milkmaids click the latch,
    And rarely smells the new-mown hay,
And the cock hath sung beneath the thatch
    Twice or thrice his roundelay,
    Twice or thrice his roundelay;
        Alone and warming his five wits,
        The white owl in the belfry sits.

LORD TENNYSON

The Donkey

When fishes flew and forests walked
And figs grew upon thorn,
Some moment when the moon was blood
Then surely I was born;

With monstrous head and sickening cry
And ears like errant wings,
The devil's walking parody
On all four-footed things.

The tattered outlaw of the earth,
Of ancient, crooked will;
Starve, scourge, deride me; I am dumb,
I keep my secret still.

Fools! For I also had my hour;
One far fierce hour and sweet:
There was a shout about my ears,
And palms before my feet.

G. K. CHESTERTON

The Kangaroo

Old Jumpety-Bumpety-Hop-and-Go-One
Was lying asleep on his side in the sun.
This old kangaroo, he was whisking the flies
(With his long glossy tail) from his ears and his
    eyes.
Jumpety-Bumpety-Hop-and-Go-One
Was lying asleep on his side in the sun,
Jumpety-Bumpety-Hop-and-Go-One.

Derby Ram

As I was going to Derby, Sir, 'twas on a
    summer's day,
I met the finest ram, Sir, that ever was fed on hay,
And indeed, Sir, 'tis true, Sir, I never was given
    to lie,
And if you'd been to Derby, Sir, you'd have seen
    him as well as I.

It had four feet to walk on, Sir, it had four feet
    to stand,
And every foot it had, Sir, did cover an acre of
    land.

*And indeed, Sir, 'tis true, Sir, I never was given
to lie,*
*And if you'd been to Derby, Sir, you'd have seen
him as well as I.*

This ram it had a horn, Sir, that reached up to
the sky,
The birds went up and built their nests, could
hear the young ones cry.
*And indeed, Sir, 'tis true, Sir, I never was given
to lie,*
*And if you'd been to Derby, Sir, you'd have seen
him as well as I.*

This ram he had another horn that reached up
to the moon,
The birds went up in January and didn't come
down till June.
*And indeed, Sir, 'tis true, Sir, I never was given
to lie,*
*And if you'd been to Derby, Sir, you'd have seen
him as well as I.*

And all the men of Derby, Sir, came begging for
his tail
To ring St George's passing-bell at the top of
Derby jail.

*And indeed, Sir, 'tis true, Sir, I never was given
to lie,*
*And if you'd been to Derby, Sir, you'd have seen
him as well as I.*

And all the women of Derby, Sir, came begging
for his ears
To make them leather aprons to last them forty
years.
*And indeed, Sir, 'tis true, Sir, I never was given
to lie,*
*And if you'd been to Derby, Sir, you'd have seen
him as well as I.*

And all the boys of Derby, Sir, came begging for
his eyes
To make a pair of footballs, for they were just
the size.
*And indeed, Sir, 'tis true, Sir, I never was given
to lie,*
*And if you'd been to Derby, Sir, you'd have seen
him as well as I.*

The butcher that killed this ram, Sir, was in
danger of his life,
He was up to his knees in blood crying out for a
longer knife.

And indeed, Sir, 'tis true, Sir, I never was given
  to lie,
And if you'd been to Derby, Sir, you'd have seen
  him as well as I.

And now my song is ended, I have no more to
  say,
So please will you give us a New Year's gift, and
  let us go away.
And indeed, Sir, 'tis true, Sir, I never was given
  to lie,
And if you'd been to Derby, Sir, you'd have seen
  him as well as I.

How Doth the Little Crocodile

How doth the little crocodile
  Improve his shining tail;
And pour the waters of the Nile
  On every golden scale!

How cheerfully he seems to grin,
  How neatly spreads his claws,
And welcomes little fishes in,
  With gently smiling jaws!

LEWIS CARROLL

Old Man Platypus

Far from the trouble and toil of town,
Where the reed-beds sweep and shiver,
Look at a fragment of velvet brown –
Old Man Platypus drifting down,
Drifting along the river.

And he plays and dives in the river bends
In a style that is most elusive;
With few relations and fewer friends,
For Old Man Platypus descends
From a family most exclusive.

He shares his burrow beneath the bank
With his wife and his son and daughter
At the roots of the reeds and the grasses rank;
And the bubbles show where our hero sank
To its entrance under water.

Safe in their burrow below the falls
They live in a world of wonder,
Where no one visits and no one calls,
They sleep like little brown billiard balls
With their beaks tucked neatly under.

And he talks in a deep unfriendly growl
As he goes on his journey lonely;
For he's no relation to fish nor fowl,
Nor to bird nor beast, nor to horned owl;
In fact, he's the one and only!

A. B. PATERSON

To a Black Greyhound

Shining black in the shining light,
Inky black in the golden sun,
Graceful as the swallow's flight,
Light as swallow, winged one,
Swift as driven hurricane,
Double-sinewed stretch and spring,
Muffled thud of flying feet –
See the black dog galloping,
Hear his wild foot-beat.

See him lie when day is dead,
Black curves curled on the boarded floor.
Sleepy eyes, my sleepy-head –
Eyes that were aflame before.
Gentle now, they burn no more;
With the fire that made them bright
Hidden – as when after storm
Softly falls the night.

JULIAN GRENFELL

The Giraffe

Hide of a leopard and hide of a deer
   And eyes of a baby calf,
Sombre and large and crystal-clear,
And a comical back that is almost sheer
   Has the absurd giraffe.

A crane all covered with hide and hair
   Is the aslant giraffe
So cleverly mottled with many a square
That even the jungle is unaware
Whether a pair or a herd is there,
   Or possibly one giraffe
   Or possibly only half.

If you saw him stoop and straddle and drink
   He would certainly make you laugh
He would certainly make you laugh, I think,
With his head right down on the water's brink,
   Would the invert giraffe,
The comical, knock-kneed, angular, crock-kneed,
   Anyhow-built giraffe.

There's more than a grain of commonsense
    And a husky lot of chaff
In the many and various arguments
    About the first giraffe,
    The first and worst giraffe:
Whether he grew a neck because
    He yearned for the higher shoots
    Out of the reach of all and each
    Of the ruminating brutes:

Or whether he got to the shoots because
His neck was long, if long it was,
    Is the cause of many disputes:
Over the ladder without any rungs
The stopper-like mouth and the longest of
    tongues
    Of the rum and dumb giraffe,
    The How-did-you-come giraffe,
The brown equatorial, semi-arboreal
    Head-in-the-air giraffe.

GEOFFREY DEARMER

From Reynard the Fox

On Ghost Heath turf was a steady drumming,
Which sounded like horses quickly coming,
It died as the hunt went down the dip,
Then Malapert yelped at Myngs's whip.
A bright iron horseshoe clinked on stone,
Then a man's voice spoke, not one alone,
Then a burst of laughter, swiftly still,
Muffled away by Ghost Heath Hill.
Then, indistinctly, the clop, clip, clep,
On Brady's Ride, of a horse's step.
Then silence, then, in a burst, much nearer,
Voices and horses coming nearer,
And another noise, of a pit-pat beat
On the Ghost Hill grass, of foxhound feet.

*   *   *

The fox was strong, he was full of running,
He could run for an hour and then be cunning,
But the cry behind him made him chill,
They were nearer now and they meant to kill.
They meant to run him until his blood
Clogged on his heart as his brush with mud,
Till his back bent up and his tongue hung
    flagging,
And his belly and brush were filthed from
    dragging.

*   *

The pure clean air came sweet to his lungs,
Till he thought foul scorn of those crying
    tongues.
In a three mile more he would reach the haven
In the Wan Dyke croaked on by the raven.
In a three mile more he would make his berth
On the cool hard floor of a Wan Dyke earth,
Too deep for spade, too curved for terrier,
With the pride of the race to make rest the
    merrier.
In a three mile more he would reach his dream,
So his game heart gulped and he put on steam.

Like a rocket shot to a ship ashore
The lean red bolt of his body tore,
Like a ripple of wind running swift on grass;
Like a shadow on wheat when a cloud blows
    past,
Like a turn at the buoy in a cutter sailing
When the bright green gleam lips white at the
    railing,
Like the April snake whipping back to sheath,
Like the gannet's hurtle on fish beneath,
Like a kestrel chasing, like a sickle reaping,
Like all things swooping, like all things sweeping,
Like a hound for stay, like a stag for swift,
With his shadow beside like spinning drift.

*   *   *

As he raced the corn towards Wan Dyke Brook
The pack had view of the way he took;
Robin hallooed from the downland's crest,
He capped them on till they did their best.
The quarter-mile to the Wan Brook's brink
Was raced as quick as a man can think.

And here, as he ran to the huntsman's yelling,
The fox first felt that the pace was telling;
His body and lungs seemed all grown old,
His legs less certain, his heart less bold,
The hound-noise nearer, the hill-slope steeper,
The thud in the blood of his body deeper.
His pride in his speed, his joy in the race,
Were withered away, for what use was pace?
He had run his best, and the hounds ran better,
Then the going worsened, the earth was wetter.
Then his brush drooped down till it sometimes
    dragged,
And his fur felt sick and his chest was tagged
With taggles of mud, and his pads seemed lead,
It was well for him he'd an earth ahead.

Down he went to the brook and over,
Out of the corn and into the clover,
Over the slope that the Wan Brook drains
Past Battle Tump where they earthed the Danes,
Then up the hill that the Wan Dyke rings
Where the Sarsen Stones stand grand like kings.

Seven Sarsens of granite grim,
As he ran them by they looked at him;
As he leaped the lip of their earthen paling.
The hounds were gaining and he was failing.

He passed the Sarsens, he left the spur,
He pressed uphill to the blasted fir,
He slipped as he leaped the hedge; he slithered.
'He's mine,' thought Robin. 'He's done; he's
    dithered.'

At the second attempt he cleared the fence,
He turned half-right where the gorse was dense,
He was leading hounds by a furlong clear.
He was past his best, but his earth was near.
He ran up gorse to the spring of the ramp,
The steep green wall of the dead men's camp,
He sidled up it and scampered down
To the deep green ditch of the Dead Men's Town.

Within, as he reached that soft green turf,
The wind, blowing lonely, moaned like surf,
Desolate ramparts rose up steep
On either side, for the ghosts to keep.
He raced the trench, past the rabbit warren,
Close-grown with moss which the wind made
    barren;
He passed the spring where the rushes spread,
And there in the stones was his earth ahead.

One last short burst upon failing feet –
There life lay waiting, so sweet, so sweet,
Rest in a darkness, balm for aches.

The earth was stopped it was barred with stakes.

With the hounds at head so close behind
He had to run as he changed his mind.
This earth, as he saw, was stopped, but still
There was one earth more on the Wan Dyke Hill –
A rabbit burrow a furlong on,
He could kennel there till the hounds were gone.
Though his death seemed near he did not blench
He upped his brush and he ran the trench.

JOHN MASEFIELD

Ducks

From troubles of the world
I turn to ducks,
Beautiful comical things
Sleeping or curled
Their heads beneath white wings
By water cool,
Or finding curious things
To eat in various mucks
Beneath the pool,

Tails uppermost, or waddling
Sailor-like on the shores
Of ponds, or paddling
– Left! right! – with fanlike feet
Which are for steady oars
When they (white galleys) float,
Each bird a boat,
Rippling at will the sweet
Wide waterway . . .

When night is fallen *you* creep
Upstairs, but drakes and dillies
Nest with pale water-stars,
Moonbeams and shadow-bars,
And water-lilies;
Fearful too much to sleep
Since they've no locks
To click against the teeth
Of weasel and fox.
And warm beneath
Are eggs of cloudy green
Whence hungry rats and lean
Would stealthily suck
New life, but for the mien,
The bold ferocious mien
Of the mother-duck.

Yes, ducks are valiant things
On nests of twigs and straws,
And ducks are soothy things
And lovely on the lake
When that the sunlight draws
Thereon their pictures dim
In colours cool.
And when beneath the pool
They dabble, and when they swim
And make their rippling rings,
O ducks are beautiful things!

But ducks are comical things –
As comical as you.
Quack!
They waddle round, they do,
They eat all sorts of things,
And then they quack.

By barn and stable and stack
They wander at their will,
But if you go too near
They look at you through black
Small topaz-tinted eyes
And wish you ill.
Triangular and clear
They leave their curious track

In mud at the water's edge,
And there amid the sedge
And slime they gobble and peer
Saying 'Quack! Quack!'

III

When God had finished the stars and whirl of
    coloured suns
He turned His mind from big things to fashion
    little ones,
Beautiful tiny things (like daisies) He made, and
    then
He made the comical ones in case the minds of
    men
      Should stiffen and become
      Dull, humourless, and glum:
And so forgetful of their Maker be
As to take even themselves – *quite seriously.*

Caterpillars and cats are lively and excellent puns:
All God's jokes are good – even the practical ones!
And as for the duck, I think God must have
    smiled a bit
Seeing those bright eyes blink on the day He
    fashioned it.
And He's probably laughing still at the sound
    that came out of its bill!

F. W. HARVEY

Christmas and the New Year

A Christmas Carol *by Christina Rossetti*   71

I Saw Three Ships Come Sailing By   72

Chester Carol – *from a Mystery Play*   72

Ring Out, Wild Bells, to the Wild Sky *by
    Lord Tennyson*   73

Wassail Song – *Old English Song*   75

A Christmas Carol

In the bleak mid-winter
   Frosty wind made moan,
Earth stood hard as iron,
   Water like a stone;
Snow had fallen, snow on snow,
   Snow on snow,
In the bleak mid-winter
   Long ago.

Our God, heaven cannot hold Him,
   Nor earth sustain;
Heaven and earth shall flee away
   When He comes to reign;
In the bleak mid-winter
   A stable-place sufficed
The Lord God Almighty
   Jesus Christ.

What can I give Him,
   Poor as I am?
If I were a shepherd
   I would bring a lamb;
If I were a wise man
   I would do my part –
Yet what I can, I give Him,
   Give my heart.

CHRISTINA ROSSETTI

I Saw Three Ships Come Sailing By

I saw three ships come sailing by,
  Come sailing by, come sailing by,
I saw three ships come sailing by,
  On New Year's day in the morning.

And what do you think was in them then,
  Was in them then, was in them then?
And what do you think was in them then,
  On New Year's day in the morning?

Three pretty girls were in them then,
  Were in them then, were in them then,
Three pretty girls were in them then,
  On New Year's Day in the morning.

One could whistle, and one could sing,
  And one could play on the violin;
Such joy there was at my wedding,
  On New Year's Day in the morning.

Chester Carol

He who made the earth so fair
Slumbers in a stable bare,
Warmed by cattle standing there.

Oxen, lowing, stand all round:
In the stall no other sound
Mars the peace by Mary found.

Joseph piles the soft, sweet hay,
Starlight drives the dark away,
Angels sing a heavenly lay.

Jesu sleeps in Mary's arm;
Sheltered there from rude alarm,
None can do Him ill or harm.

See His mother o'er Him bend;
Hers the joy to soothe and tend,
Hers the bliss that knows no end.

FROM A CHESTER MYSTERY PLAY

Ring Out, Wild Bells, to the Wild Sky

Ring out, wild bells, to the wild sky,
  The flying cloud, the frosty light:
  The year is dying in the night:
Ring out, wild bells, and let him die.

Ring out the old, ring in the new,
  Ring, happy bells, across the snow:
  The year is going, let him go;
Ring out the false, ring in the true.

Ring out the grief that saps the mind,
   For those that here we see no more;
   Ring out the feud of rich and poor,
Ring in redress to all mankind.

Ring out the want, the care, the sin,
   The faithless coldness of the times;
   Ring out, ring out my mournful rhymes,
But ring the fuller minstrel in.

Ring out false pride in place and blood,
   The civic slander and the spite;
   Ring in the love of truth and right,
Ring in the common love of good.

Ring out old shapes of foul disease;
   Ring out the narrowing lust of gold;
   Ring out the thousand wars of old,
Ring in the thousand years of peace.

Ring in the valiant man and free,
   The larger heart, the kindlier hand;
   Ring out the darkness of the land,
Ring in the Christ that is to be.

LORD TENNYSON

Wassail Song

Here we come a-wassailing
  Among the leaves so green,
Here we come a-wandering,
  So fair to be seen.

    Love and joy come to you,
    And to you your wassail too,
    And God bless you, and send you
    A happy new year.

We are not daily beggars
  That beg from door to door,
But we are neighbours' children
  Whom you have seen before.

God bless the master of this house,
  Likewise the mistress too;
And all the little children
  That round the table go;

And all your kin and kinsfolk,
  That dwell both far and near;
We wish you a Merry Christmas,
  And a Happy New Year.

OLD ENGLISH SONG

Landscapes and Seasons

Flower in the Crannied Wall *by Lord Tennyson* 77
Spring Song *by William Blake* 77
The Garden Year *by Sara Coleridge* 78
I Wandered Lonely as a Cloud *by William Wordsworth* 79
The Way Through the Woods *by Rudyard Kipling* 80
Written in March *by William Wordsworth* 81
Home Thoughts from Abroad *by Robert Browning* 82
The Storm *by Walter de la Mare* 83
Lines Composed in a Wood on a Windy Day *by Anne Brontë* 85
Morning after a Storm *by William Wordsworth* 86
The Tide Rises, the Tide Falls *by H. W. Longfellow* 86
Boats Sail on the Rivers *by Christina Rossetti* 87
Sampler *by Howard Sergeant* 88
Miracles *by Walt Whitman* 88

Flower in the Crannied Wall

Flower in the crannied wall,
I pluck you out of the crannies,
I hold you here, root and all, in my hand,
Little flower – but if I could understand
What you are, root and all, and all in all,
I should know what God and man is.

LORD TENNYSON

Spring Song

Spring is coming, spring is coming,
  Birdies, build your nest;
Weave together straw and feather,
  Doing each your best.

Spring is coming, spring is coming,
  Flowers are coming too;
Pansies, lilies, daffodillies
  Now are coming through.

Spring is coming, spring is coming,
  All around is fair,
Shimmer and quiver on the river,
  Joy is everywhere.

WILLIAM BLAKE

The Garden Year

January brings the snow,
Makes our feet and fingers glow.

February brings the rain,
Thaws the frozen lake again.

March brings breezes, loud and shrill,
To stir the dancing daffodil.

April brings the primrose sweet,
Scatters daisies at our feet.

May brings flocks of pretty lambs,
Skipping by their fleecy dams.

June brings tulips, lilies, roses,
Fills the children's hands with posies.

Hot July brings cooling showers,
Apricots and gillyflowers.

August brings the sheaves of corn,
Then the harvest home is borne.

Warm September brings the fruit;
Sportsmen then begin to shoot.

Fresh October brings the pheasant;
Then to gather nuts is pleasant.

Dull November brings the blast;
Then the leaves are whirling fast.

Chill December brings the sleet,
Blazing fire, and Christmas treat.

SARA COLERIDGE

I Wandered Lonely as a Cloud

I wandered lonely as a cloud
That floats on high o'er vale and hills,
When all at once I saw a crowd,
A host, of golden daffodils;
Beside the lake, beneath the trees,
Fluttering and dancing in the breeze.

Continuous as the stars that shine
And twinkle on the Milky Way,
They stretched in never-ending line
Along the margin of a bay:
Ten thousand saw I at a glance,
Tossing their heads in sprightly dance.

The waves beside them danced; but they
Out-did the sparkling waves in glee:
A poet could not but be gay
In such a jocund company:
I gazed – and gazed – but little thought
What wealth the show to me had brought.

For oft, when on my couch I lie
In vacant or in pensive mood,
They flash upon that inward eye
Which is the bliss of solitude;
And then my heart with pleasure fills,
And dances with the daffodils.

WILLIAM WORDSWORTH

The Way Through the Woods

They shut the road through the woods
Seventy years ago.
Weather and rain have undone it again,
And now you would never know
There once was a road through the woods
Before they planted the trees.
It is underneath the coppice and heath,
And the thin anemones.
Only the keeper sees
That, where the ring-dove broods,
And the badgers roll at ease,
There once was a way through the woods.

Yet, if you enter the woods
Of a summer evening late,
When the night air cools on the trout-ringed
    pools
Where the otter whistles his mate,
(They fear not men in the woods,
Because they see so few)
You will hear the beat of a horse's feet,
And the swish of a skirt in the dew,
Steadily cantering through
The misty solitudes,
As though they perfectly knew
The old lost road through the woods . . .
But there is no road through the woods!

RUDYARD KIPLING

Written in March

The cock is crowing,
The stream is flowing,
The small birds twitter,
The lake doth glitter,
The green field sleeps in the sun;
The oldest and youngest
Are at work with the strongest;
The cattle are grazing,
Their heads never raising;
There are forty feeding like one!

Like an army defeated
The snow hath retreated,
And now doth fare ill
On the top of the bare hill;
The ploughboy is whooping – anon – anon:
There's joy in the mountains;
There's life in the fountains;
Small clouds are sailing,
Blue sky prevailing;
The rain is over and gone!

WILLIAM WORDSWORTH

Home Thoughts, from Abroad

Oh, to be in England
Now that April's there,
And whoever wakes in England
Sees, some morning unaware,
That the lowest boughs and the brushwood sheaf
Round the elm-tree bole are in tiny leaf,
While the chaffinch sings on the orchard bough
In England – now!

And after April, when May follows,
And the whitethroat builds, and all the swallows!
Hark, where my blossomed pear-tree in the
     hedge
Leans to the field and scatters on the clover
Blossoms and dewdrops – at the bent spray's edge –

That's the wise thrush; he sings each song twice
    over,
Lest you should think he never could recapture
The first fine careless rapture!
And though the fields look rough with hoary
    dew,
All will be gay when noontide wakes anew
The buttercups, the little children's dower.
– Far brighter than this gaudy melon-flower.

ROBERT BROWNING

The Storm

First there were two of us, then there were three
    of us,
Then there was one bird more,
Four of us – wild white sea-birds,
Treading the ocean floor;
And the wind rose, and the sea rose,
To the angry billows' roar –
With one of us – two of us – three of us – four
    of us
Sea-birds on the shore.

Soon there were five of us, soon there were nine
    of us,
And lo! in a trice sixteen!
And the yeasty surf curdled over the sands,
The gaunt grey rocks between;

And the tempest raved, and the lightning's fire
Struck blue on the spindrift hoar –
And on four of us – ay, and on four times four
  of us
Sea-birds on the shore.

And our sixteen waxed to thirty-two,
And they to past three score
A wild, white welter of winnowing wings,
And ever more and more;
And the winds lulled, and the sea went down,
And the sun streamed out on high,
Gilding the pools and the spume and the spars
'Neath the vast blue deeps of the sky.

And the isles and the bright green headlands
  shone,
As they never shone before,
Mountains and valleys of silver cloud,
Wherein to swing, sweep, soar –
A host of screeching, scolding, scrabbling,
Sea-birds on the shore –
A snowy, silent, sunwashed drift
Of sea-birds on the shore.

WALTER DE LA MARE

Lines Composed in a Wood on a Windy Day

My soul is awakened, my spirit is soaring
And carried aloft on the wings of the breeze;
For above and around me the wild wind is
    roaring,
Arousing to rapture the earth and the seas.

The long withered grass in the sunshine is
    glancing,
The bare trees are tossing their branches on high;
The dead leaves, beneath them, are merrily
    dancing,
The white clouds are scudding across the blue sky.

I wish I could see how the ocean is lashing
The foam of its billows to whirlwinds of spray;
I wish I could see how its proud waves are
    dashing,
And hear the wild roar of their thunder today.

ANNE BRONTË

Morning after a Storm

There was a roaring in the wind all night;
The rain came heavily and fell in floods;
But now the sun is rising calm and bright;
The birds are singing in the distant woods;
Over his own sweet voice the stock-dove broods;
The jay makes answer as the magpie chatters;
And all the air is filled with pleasant noise of waters.

All things that love the sun are out of doors;
The sky rejoices in the morning's birth;
The grass is bright with raindrops – on the
    moors
The hare is running races in her mirth;
And with her feet she from the plashy earth
Raises a mist, that, glittering in the sun,
Runs with her all the way, wherever she doth run.

WILLIAM WORDSWORTH

The Tide Rises, the Tide Falls

The tide rises, the tide falls,
The twilight darkens, the curlew calls,
Along the sea-sands damp and brown
The traveller hastens toward the town;
   And the tide rises, the tide falls.

Darkness settles on roof and walls,
But the sea in the darkness calls and calls;
The little waves, with their soft white hands,
Efface the footprints in the sands,
    And the tide rises, the tide falls.

The morning breaks; the steeds in their stalls
Stamp and neigh, as the hostler calls;
The day returns; but nevermore
Returns the traveller to the shore,
    And the tide rises, the tide falls.

H. W. LONGFELLOW

Boats Sail on the Rivers

Boats sail on the rivers,
    And ships sail on the seas;
But clouds that sail across the sky
    Are prettier far than these.

There are bridges on the rivers,
    As pretty as you please;
But the bow that bridges heaven,
    And overtops the trees,
And builds a road from earth to sky,
    Is prettier far than these.

CHRISTINA ROSSETTI

Sampler

Here where the kittiwakes idle
On the coolest drills and checks,
The sun, sharp as a needle,
Sews ribbons round their necks.

And where the tweedy beeches
Are buttoned up with glass,
In long-armed feather-stitches
Marries sand and marram grass.

HOWARD SERGEANT

Miracles

Why, who makes much of a miracle?
As to me I know of nothing else but miracles,
Whether I walk the streets of Manhattan,
Or dart my sight over the roofs of houses toward
    the sky,
Or wade with naked feet along the beach just in
    the edge of the water,
Or stand under trees in the woods,
Or watch honey-bees busy around the hives of a
    summer forenoon,
Or animals feeding in the fields,
Or birds, or the wonderfulness of insects in the air,

Or the wonderfulness of the sundown, or of
    stars shining so quiet and bright,
Or the exquisite delicate thin curve of the new
    moon in spring;
These with the rest, one and all, are to me
    miracles.
The whole referring, yet each distinct and in its
    place.

To me every hour of the light and dark is a
    miracle,
Every cubic inch of space is a miracle,
Every square yard of the surface of the earth is
    spread with the same,
Every foot of the interior swarms with the same.

To me the sea is a continual miracle,
The fishes that swim – the rocks – the motion of
    the waves – the ships with men in them,
What stranger miracles are there?

WALT WHITMAN

Types and Conditions of Man

Legend *by Judith Wright*   91

A Man of Words   93

The Pilgrim *by John Bunyan*   94

The Land of Counterpane *by Robert Louis Stevenson*   95

Under the Greenwood Tree *by William Shakespeare*   96

There Was a Man   97

Gipsies *by John Clare*   97

I Remember, *by Thomas Hood*   98

Legend

The blacksmith's boy went out with a rifle
And a black dog running behind.
Cobwebs snatched at his feet,
Rivers hindered him,
Thorn-branches caught at his eyes to make him
    blind
And the sky turned into an unlucky opal,
But he didn't mind.
I can break branches, I can swim rivers, I can
    stare out any spider I meet,
Said he to his dog and his rifle.

The blacksmith's boy went over the paddocks
With his old black hat on his head.
Mountains jumped in his way,
Rocks rolled down on him,
And the old crow cried, *You'll soon be dead;*
And the rain came down like mattocks.
But he only said
I can climb mountains, I can dodge rocks, I can
    shoot an old crow any day.
And he went on over the paddocks.

When he came to the end of the day the sun
  began falling.
Up came the night ready to swallow him,
Like the barrel of a gun,
Like an old black hat,
Like a black dog hungry to follow him.
Then the pigeon, the magpie and the dove
  began wailing,
And the grass lay down to pillow him.
His rifle broke, his hat blew away and his dog
  was gone,
And the sun was falling.

But in front of the night the rainbow stood out
  on the mountain
Just as his heart foretold.
He ran like a hare,
He climbed like a fox,
He caught it in his hands, the colours and the
  cold –
Like a bar of ice, like the columns of a fountain,
Like a ring of gold.
The pigeon, the magpie and the dove flew up to
  stare,
And the grass stood up again on the mountain.

The blacksmith's boy hung the rainbow on his
  shoulder,
Instead of his broken gun.

Lizards ran out to see,
Snakes made way for him,
And the rainbow shone as brightly as the sun.
All the world said, *Nobody is braver, nobody is
    bolder*,
Nobody else has done
Anything to equal it. He went home as easy as
    could be
With the swinging rainbow on his shoulder.

JUDITH WRIGHT

A Man of Words

A man of words and not of deeds
Is like a garden full of weeds.

When the weeds begin to grow,
It's like a garden full of snow.

When the snow begins to fall,
It's like a bird upon the wall;

When the bird begins to fly,
It's like an eagle in the sky;

When the sky begins to roar,
It's like a lion at the door;

When the door begins to crack,
It's like a whip across your back;

When your back begins to smart,
It's like a penknife in your heart;

And when your heart begins to bleed,
You're dead, you're dead, you're dead indeed.

The Pilgrim

Who would true valour see,
   Let him come hither!
One here will constant be
   Come wind, come weather;
There's no discouragement
Shall make him once relent
His first-avowed intent
   To be a Pilgrim.

Whoso beset him round
   With dismal stories,
Do but themselves confound;
   His strength the more is.
No lion can him fright;
He'll with a giant fight;
But he will have the right
   To be a Pilgrim.

Hobgoblin, nor foul fiend,
   Can daunt his spirit;
He knows he at the end
   Shall Life inherit:
Then fancies fly away;
He'll not fear what men say;
He'll labour, night and day,
   To be a Pilgrim.

JOHN BUNYAN

The Land of Counterpane

When I was sick and lay a-bed,
I had two pillows at my head,
And all my toys beside me lay,
To keep me happy all the day.

And sometimes for an hour or so
I watched my leaden soldiers go,
With different uniforms and drills,
Among the bedclothes, through the hills;

And sometimes sent my ships in fleets
All up and down among the sheets;
Or brought my trees and houses out,
And planted cities all about.

I was the giant great and still
That sits upon the pillow-hill,
And sees before him, dale and plain,
The pleasant land of counterpane.

ROBERT LOUIS STEVENSON

Under the Greenwood Tree

Under the greenwood tree
Who loves to lie with me,
And tune his merry note
Unto the sweet bird's throat,
　Come hither, come hither, come hither;
Here shall he see
No enemy
　But winter and rough weather.

Who doth ambition shun,
And loves to live in the sun,
Seeking the food he eats,
And pleased with what he gets,

Come hither, come hither, come hither:
Here shall he see
No enemy
But winter and rough weather.

WILLIAM SHAKESPEARE

There Was a Man

There was a man, and he had nought,
    And robbers came to rob him;
He crept up into the chimney-pot
    And then they thought they had him.

But he got down on t'other side.
    And then they could not find him,
He ran fourteen miles in fifteen days,
    And never looked behind him.

Gipsies

The gipsies seek wide sheltering woods again,
With droves of horses flock to mark their lane,
And trample on dead leaves, and hear the sound,
And look and see the black clouds gather round,
And set their camps, and free from muck and
        mire,
And gather stolen sticks to make the fire,

The roasted hedgehog, bitter though as gall,
Is eaten up and relished by them all.
They know the woods and every fox's den
And get their living far away from men;
The shooters ask them where to find the game,
The rabbits know them and are almost tame.
The aged women, tawny with the smoke,
Go with the winds and crack the rotted oak.

JOHN CLARE

I Remember

I remember, I remember,
The house where I was born,
The little window, where the sun
Came peeping in at morn:
He never came a wink too soon,
Nor brought too long a day,
But now I often wish the night
Had borne my breath away!

I remember, I remember,
The roses, red and white,
The violets, and the lily-cups.
Those flowers made of light!
The lilacs, where the robin built,
And where my brother set
The laburnum on his birthday:
The tree is living yet!

I remember, I remember,
Where I was used to swing,
And thought the air must rush as fresh
To swallows on the wing.
My spirit flew in feathers then,
That is so heavy now;
And summer pools could hardly cool
The fever on my brow!

I remember, I remember,
The fir-trees, dark and high;
I used to think their slender tops
Were close against the sky:
It was a childish ignorance:
But now, 'tis little joy
To know I'm farther off from heaven
Than when I was a boy.

THOMAS HOOD

Battles Lost and Won

The Coasts of High Barbary – *Folk Song*   101

A Knight and a Lady   103

The War Song of Dinas Vawr *by Thomas Love Peacock*   104

The Charge of the Light Brigade *by Lord Tennyson*   105

King Henry V at the Battle of Agincourt *by William Shakespeare*   108

Dunkirk 1940 *by Idris Davies*   109

The Coasts of High Barbary

Look ahead, look astern, look the weather and
      the lee;
  Blow high! Blow low! and so sailed we;
I see a wreck to windward and a lofty ship to lee,
  *A-sailing down all on the coasts of High
      Barbary.*

'Then hail her,' our captain he called o'er the
      side;
  Blow high! Blow low! and so sailed we;
'O are you a pirate or a man-o'-war?' he cried,
  *A-sailing down all on the coasts of High
      Barbary.*

'O are you a pirate or man-o'-war?' cried we;
  Blow high! Blow low! and so sailed we;
'O no! I'm not a pirate but a man-o'-war,' cried he.
  *A-sailing down all on the coasts of High
      Barbary.*

'Then back up your top-sails, and heave your
      vessel to,'
  Blow high! Blow low! and so sailed we;
'For we have got some letters to be carried home
  by you,'
  *A-sailing down all on the coasts of High
      Barbary.*

'We'll back up our top-sails and heave our
        vessel to;'
  Blow high! Blow low! and so sailed we;
'But only in some harbour and along the side of you:'
  *A-sailing down all on the coasts of High
        Barbary.*

For broadside, for broadside, they fought all on
        the main;
  Blow high! Blow low! and so sailed we;
Until at last the frigate shot the pirate's mast away;
  *A-sailing down all on the coasts of High
        Barbary.*

'For quarters! for quarters!' the saucy pirates cried;
  Blow high! Blow low! and so sailed we;
The quarters that we showed them was to sink
        them in the tide;
  *A-sailing down all on the coasts of High
        Barbary.*

With cutlass and gun O we fought for hours
        three;
  Blow high! Blow low! and so sailed we;
The ship it was their coffin, and their grave it
        was the sea;
  *A-sailing down all on the coasts of High
        Barbary.*

But O it was a cruel sight and grievèd us full sore,
Blow high! Blow low! and so sailed we;
To see them all a-drowning as they tried to swim
to shore;
*A-sailing down all on the coasts of High
Barbary.*

FOLK SONG

A Knight and a Lady

A knight and a lady
Went riding one day
Far into the forest,
Away, away.

'Fair knight,' said the lady,
'I pray, have a care.
This forest is evil –
Beware, beware!'

A fiery red dragon
They spied on the grass;
The lady wept sorely,
Alas! Alas!

The knight slew the dragon,
The lady was gay.
They rode on together,
Away, away.

The War Song of Dinas Vawr

The mountain sheep are sweeter,
But the valley sheep are fatter;
We therefore deemed it meeter
To carry off the latter.
We made an expedition;
We met a host, and quelled it;
We forced a strong position,
And killed the men who held it.

On Dyfed's richest valley,
Where herds of kine were brousing,
We made a mighty sally,
To furnish our carousing.
Fierce warriors rushed to meet us;
We met them, and o'erthrew them:
They struggled hard to beat us;
But we conquered them, and slew them.

And we drove our prize at leisure,
The king marched forth to catch us:
His rage surpassed all measure,
But his people could not match us.
He fled to his hall-pillars;
And ere our force we led off,
Some sacked his house and cellars,
While others cut his head off.

We there, in strife bewildering,
Spilt blood enough to swim in:
We orphaned many children,
And widowed many women.
The eagles and the ravens
We glutted with our foemen;
The heroes and the cravens,
The spearmen and the bowmen.

We brought away from battle,
And much their land bemoaned them,
Two thousand head of cattle,
And the head of him who owned them:
Ednyfed, King of Dyfed,
His head was borne before us;
His wine and beasts supplied our feasts,
And his overthrow, our chorus.

THOMAS LOVE PEACOCK

The Charge of the Light Brigade

Half a league, half a league,
Half a league onward,
All in the valley of Death
Rode the six hundred.
'Forward, the Light Brigade!
Charge for the guns!' he said;
Into the valley of Death
Rode the six hundred.

'Forward the Light Brigade!'
Was there a man dismayed?
Not though the soldier knew
Someone had blundered:
Their's not to make reply,
Their's not to reason why,
Their's but to do and die:
Into the valley of Death
Rode the six hundred.

Cannon to right of them,
Cannon to left of them,
Cannon in front of them
Volleyed and thundered;
Stormed at with shot and shell,
Boldly they rode and well,
Into the jaws of Death,
Into the mouth of Hell
Rode the six hundred.

Flashed all their sabres bare,
Flashed as they turned in air,
Sabring the gunners there,
Charging an army, while
All the world wondered:
Plunged in the battery-smoke
Right through the line they broke;
Cossack and Russian

Reeled from the sabre-stroke
Shattered and sundered.
Then they rode back, but not,
Not the six hundred.

Cannon to right of them,
Cannon to left of them,
Cannon behind them
Volleyed and thundered;
Stormed at with shot and shell,
While horse and hero fell,
They that had fought so well
Came through the jaws of Death
Back from the mouth of Hell,
All that was left of them,
Left of six hundred.

When can their glory fade?
O the wild charge they made!
All the world wondered.
Honour the charge they made!
Honour the Light Brigade,
Noble six hundred.

LORD TENNYSON

King Henry V at the Battle of Agincourt

This day is called the feast of Crispian.
He that outlives this day, and comes safe home,
Will stand a tip-toe when this day is named,
And rouse him at the name of Crispian.
He that shall live this day, and see old age,
Will yearly on the vigil feast his neighbours,
And say, 'Tomorrow is Saint Crispian.'
Then will he strip his sleeve and show his scars,
And say, 'These wounds I had on Crispian's day.'
Old men forget; yet all shall be forgot,
But he'll remember, with advantages,
What feats he did that day. Then shall our names,
Familiar in his mouth as household words –
Harry the King, Bedford and Exeter,
Warwick and Talbot, Salisbury and Gloucester –
Be in their flowing cups freshly remembered.

This story shall the good man teach his son;
And Crispin Crispian shall ne'er go by,
From this day to the ending of the world,
But we in it shall be remembered –
We few, we happy few, we band of brothers;
For he today that sheds his blood with me
Shall be my brother; be he ne'er so vile.
This day shall gentle his condition;
And gentlemen in England now a-bed

Shall think themselves accursed they were not here,
And hold their manhoods cheap while any speaks,
That fought with us upon Saint Crispian's day.

WILLIAM SHAKESPEARE

Dunkirk, 1940

The little ships, the little ships
  Rushed out across the sea
To save the luckless armies
  From death and slavery.

From Tyne and Thames and Tamar,
  From the Severn and the Clyde,
The little ships, the little ships
  Went out in all their pride.

And home they brought their warriors,
  Weary and ragged and worn,
Back to the hills and shires
  And the towns where they were born.

Three hundred thousand warriors,
  From Hell to Home they came,
In the little ships, the little ships
  Of everlasting fame.

IDRIS DAVIES

Man's Endless Quest

When a Man hath no Freedom to Fight for
   at Home *by Lord Byron*   III

Precious Stones *by Christina Rossetti*   III

Looking at Stars *by Phoebe Hesketh*   II2

Hurt No Living Thing *by Christina Rossetti*   II2

Fear No More the Heat o' the Sun *by
   William Shakespeare*   II3

Upon Westminster Bridge *by William
   Wordsworth*   II4

Rocket to the Moon *by Douglas Gibson*   II5

Uphill *by Christina Rossetti*   II6

When a Man hath no Freedom to Fight for at Home

When a man hath no freedom to fight for at
      home,
   Let him combat for that of his neighbours;
Let him think of the glories of Greece and of
      Rome,
   And get knocked on the head for his labours.

To do good to mankind is the chivalrous plan,
   And is always as nobly requited;
Then battle for Freedom wherever you can
   And, if not shot or hanged, you'll get knighted.

LORD BYRON

Precious Stones

An emerald is as green as grass,
   A ruby red as blood,
A sapphire shines as blue as heaven,
   But a flint lies in the mud.

A diamond is a brilliant stone
   To catch the world's desire,
An opal holds a rainbow light,
   But a flint holds fire.

CHRISTINA ROSSETTI

Looking at Stars

I know the stars, remote and bright,
That pierce the backcloth of the night.
But they look down, blind, unaware
Of one immortal watcher there.

Through space and time, light-years apart,
They whirl above our dust and die,
Oblivious that a mortal heart
Is charged with immortality.

I seek for truth behind those eyes,
But lost in darkening gulfs of space,
Return to the light before my face,
For I have greatness without size.

PHOEBE HESKETH

Hurt No Living Thing

Hurt no living thing;
Ladybird, nor butterfly,
Nor moth with dusty wing,
Nor cricket chirping cheerily,
Nor grasshopper so light of leap,
Nor dancing gnat, nor beetle fat,
Nor harmless worms that creep.

CHRISTINA ROSSETTI

Fear No More the Heat o' the Sun

Fear no more the heat o' the sun,
  Nor the furious winter's rages;
Thou thy worldly task hast done,
  Home art gone, and ta'en thy wages.
Golden lads and girls all must,
As chimney-sweepers, come to dust.

Fear no more the frown o' the great,
  Thou art past the tyrant's stroke;
Care no more to clothe and eat,
  To thee the reed is as the oak.
The sceptre, learning, physic, must,
All follow this, and come to dust.

Fear no more the lightning-flash,
  Nor all the all-dreaded thunder-stone:
Fear not slander, censure rash;
  Thou hast finished joy and moan.
All lovers young, all lovers must
Consign to thee, and come to dust.

WILLIAM SHAKESPEARE

Upon Westminster Bridge
September 3, 1802.

Earth has not anything to show more fair:
Dull would he be of soul who could pass by
A sight so touching in its majesty:
This city now doth like a garment wear

The beauty of the morning: silent, bare,
Ships, towers, domes, theatres, and temples lie
Open unto the fields, and to the sky –
All bright and glittering in the smokeless air.

Never did sun more beautifully steep
In his first splendour valley, rock or hill;
Ne'er saw I, never felt, a calm so deep!

The river glideth at his own sweet will:
Dear God! the very houses seem asleep;
And all that mighty heart is lying still!

WILLIAM WORDSWORTH

Rocket to the Moon

The moon betrays no recognition
Of this success: remote and white,
Unawed by restless man's ambition,
It pours the sun's reflected light
On cities, meadows, mountains, seas,
And some enchanted by its charms
Under the silver-dappled trees
Move closer in each other's arms.

Undreamt till now, it seems that soon,
Launched into space, a man may be
Upon the dead world of the moon
Where no air is, no flowers, no sea,
Nothing our mortal hearts desire,
Only the quest that made us come
Out of the dark, through ice and fire,
To learn a voice who once were dumb.

DOUGLAS GIBSON

Uphill

Does the road wind uphill all the way?
    Yes, to the very end.
Will the day's journey take the whole day long?
    From morn to night, my friend.

But is there for the night a resting-place?
    A roof for when the slow, dark hours begin.
May not the darkness hide it from my face?
    You cannot miss that inn.

Shall I meet other wayfarers at night?
    Those who have gone before.
Then must I knock, or call when just in sight?
    They will not keep you waiting at the door.

Shall I find comfort, travel-sore and weak?
    Of labour you shall find the sum.
Will there be beds for me and all who seek?
    Yea, beds for all who come.

CHRISTINA ROSSETTI

Night-time and Dreams

Escape at Bedtime *by Robert Louis Stevenson*   118
The Land of Nod *by Robert Louis Stevenson*   119
Dream-Pedlary by *Thomas Lovell Beddoes*   120
Bed in Summer *by Robert Louis Stevenson*   121
Jack Frost *by Gabriel Setoun*   122
Lights Out *by Edward Thomas*   123

Escape at Bedtime

The lights from the parlour and kitchen shone out
   Through the blinds and the windows and bars;
And high overhead and all moving about,
   There were thousands of millions of stars.
There ne'er were such thousands of leaves on a
      tree,
   Nor of people in church or the park,
As the crowds of the stars that looked down on me,
   And that glittered and winked in the dark.
The Dog and the Plough, and the Hunter, and
      all,
   And the star of the sailor, and Mars,
These shone in the sky, and the pail by the wall
   Would be half full of water and stars.
They saw me at last, and they chased me with
      cries,
   And they soon had me packed into bed;
But the glory kept shining and bright in my eyes,
   And the stars going round in my head.

ROBERT LOUIS STEVENSON

The Land of Nod

From breakfast on through all the day
At home among my friends I stay,
But every night I go abroad
Afar into the Land of Nod.

All by myself I have to go,
With none to tell me what to do –
All alone beside the streams
And up the mountain-sides of dreams.

The strangest things are there for me,
Both things to eat and things to see,
And many frightening sights abroad.
Till morning in the land of Nod.

Try as I like to find the way,
I never can get back by day,
Nor can remember plain and clear
The curious music that I hear.

ROBERT LOUIS STEVENSON

Dream-Pedlary

If there were dreams to sell,
　　What would you buy?
Some cost a passing bell;
　　Some a light sigh,
That shakes from Life's fresh crown
Only a rose-leaf down.
If there were dreams to sell,
Merry and sad to tell,
And the crier rung the bell,
　　What would you buy?

A cottage lone and still,
　　With bowers nigh,
Shadowy, my woes to still,
　　Until I die.
Such pearl from Life's fresh crown
Fain would I shake me down.
Were dreams to have at will,
This would best heal my ill,
　　This would I buy.

But there were dreams to sell
  Ill didst thou buy;
Life is a dream, they tell,
  Waking, to die.
Dreaming – a dream to prize –
Is wishing ghosts to rise;
And, if I had the spell
To call the buried, well,
  Which one would I?

THOMAS LOVELL BEDDOES

Bed in Summer

In winter I get up at night
And dress by yellow candle-light.
In summer, quite the other way,
I have to go to bed by day.

I have to go to bed and see
The birds still hopping on the tree,
Or hear the grown-up people's feet
Still going past me in the street.

And does it not seem hard to you,
When all the sky is clear and blue,
And I should like so much to play,
To have to go to bed by day?

ROBERT LOUIS STEVENSON

Jack Frost

The door was shut, as doors should be,
  Before you went to bed last night;
Yet Jack Frost has got in, you see,
  And left your window silver white.

He must have waited till you slept;
  And not a single word he spoke;
But pencilled o'er the panes and crept
  Away again before you woke.

And here are little boats, and there
  Big ships with sails spread to the breeze;
And yonder, palm trees waving fair
  On islands set in silver seas.

And butterflies with gauzy wings;
  And herds of cows and flocks of sheep;
And fruit and flowers and all the things
  You see when you are sound asleep.

And now you cannot see the hills
  Nor fields that stretch beyond the lane;
But there are fairer things than these
  His fingers traced on every pane.

Rocks and castles towering high;
  Hills and dales and streams and fields;
And knights in armour riding by,
  With nodding plumes and shining shields.

For creeping softly underneath
  The door when all the lights are out,
Jack Frost takes every breath you breathe,
  And knows the things you think about.

He paints them on the window pane
  In fairy lines with frozen steam;
And when you wake you see again
  The lovely things you saw in dream.

GABRIEL SETOUN

Lights Out

I have come to the borders of sleep,
The unfathomable deep
Forest where all must lose
Their way, however straight,
Or winding, soon or late;
They cannot choose.

123

Many a road and track
That, since the dawn's first crack,
Up to the forest brink,
Deceived the travellers,
Suddenly now blurs,
And in they sink.

Here love ends,
Despair, ambition ends,
All pleasure and all trouble,
Although most sweet or bitter,
Here ends in sleep that is sweeter
Than tasks most noble.

There is not any book
Or face of dearest look
That I would not turn from now
To go into the unknown
I must enter and leave alone
I know not how.

The tall forest towers;
Its cloudy foliage lowers
Ahead, shelf above shelf;
Its silence I hear and obey
That I may lose my way
And myself.

EDWARD THOMAS

Index of Authors

Beddoes, Thomas Lovell, 120
Blake, William, 77
Bloomfield, Robert, 39
Brontë, Anne, 85
Browning, Robert, 82
Bunyan, John, 94
Byron, Lord, 111

Carroll, Lewis, 42, 57
Chesterton, G. K., 53
Clare, John, 47, 97
Coleridge, Sara, 78
Coleridge, Samuel Taylor, 15

Davies, Idris, 109
Dearmer, Geoffrey, 60
De la Mare, Walter, 83

Eliot, T. S., 49

Gibson, Douglas, 115
Grenfell, Julian, 59

Harvey, F. W., 66
Hesketh, Phoebe, 112
Hood, Thomas, 38, 98

Kipling, Rudyard, 80

Lear, Edward, 34
Longfellow, H. W., 86

Masefield, John, 62

Paterson, A. B., 58
Peacock, Thomas Love, 104

Rossetti, Christina, 48, 71, 87,
   111, 112, 116

Sergeant, Howard, 88
Setoun, Gabriel, 122
Shakespeare, William, 32, 96,
   108, 113
Stevenson, Robert Louis, 95,
   118, 119, 121
Swift, Jonathan, 16

Tennyson, Lord, 52, 73, 77,
   105
Thomas, Edward, 123

Whitman, Walt, 88
Wordsworth, William, 79, 81,
   86, 114
Wright, Judith, 91

Index of First Lines

A fox jumped up one winter's night,   26
A knight and a lady   103
A little cock sparrow sat on a tree,   11
A man of words and not of deeds   93
An emerald is as green as grass,   111
A silly young cricket, accustomed to sing   44
As I was going to Derby, Sir, 'twas on a summer's day,   54
As I was going up the stair   12

Boats sail on the rivers,   87

Does the road wind uphill all the way?   116
Don't-Care – he didn't care,   14
Down in the meadow   20
Do you ask what the birds say? The sparrow and the dove,   15

Eaper, weaper, chimbley-sweeper,   11
Earth has not anything to show more fair: 114

Far from the trouble and toil of town,   58
Fear no more the heat o' the sun,   113
Fire in the galley, fire down below,   19
First there were two of us, then there were three of us,   83
Flower in the crannied wall,   77
From breakfast on through all the day   119
From troubles of the world   66

Guy Fawkes, Guy!   21

Half a league, half a league,   105
Here we come a-wassailing   75
Here where the kittiwakes idle   88
He thought he saw an Elephant,   42
He who made the earth so fair   72
Hide of a leopard and hide of a deer   60
How doth the little crocodile   57
How many miles to Babylon?   16
Hurt no living thing;   112

If there were dreams to sell,   120

I have come to the borders of sleep,   123
I know the stars, remote and bright,   112
In the bleak mid-winter   71
In the cowslip pips I lie,   47
In winter I get up at night   121
I remember, I remember,   98
I saw three ships come sailing by,   72
I wandered lonely as a cloud   79

January brings the snow,   78

Little Jack Horner   10
London Bridge is broken down   24
Look ahead, look astern, look the weather and the lee;   101

Macavity's a Mystery Cat; he's called the Hidden Paw –   49
Mary, Mary, quite contrary,   11
Monday's child is fair of face,   10
My soul is awakened, my spirit is soaring   85

Oh! Soldier, soldier, won't you marry me,   31
Old Jumpety-Bumpety-Hop-and-Go-One   54
Oh, to be in England   82
Old Noah once built the ark,   28
Old Roger is dead and gone to his grave,   18
On Ghost Heath turf was a steady drumming   62
O, the grand old Duke of York   14
Our old cat has kittens three –   38

Ring out, wild bells, to the wild sky,   73

Shining black in the shining light,   59
Sing a song of sixpence,   12
Spring is coming, spring is coming,   77

The blacksmith's boy went out with a rifle   91
The door was shut, as doors should be,   122
The cock is crowing,   81
The earth was green, the sky was blue: 48
The gipsies seek wide sheltering woods again,   97
The horses of the sea   48
The lawns were dry in Euston park: 39
The lights from the parlour and kitchen shone out   118

The little ships, the little ships,   109
The moon betrays no recognition   115
The mountain sheep are sweeter,   104
The tide rises, the tide falls,   86
There came three men from out the West   22
There was a crooked man, and   13
There was a man, and he had nought,   97
There was an old woman who lived in a shoe,   13
There was a roaring in the wind all night;   86
They shut the road through the woods   80
They went to sea in a Sieve, they did,   34
This day is called the feast of Crispian,   108

We are very little creatures,   16
When a man hath no freedom to fight for at home,   111
When cats run home and light is come,   52
When fishes flew and forests walked   53
When icicles hang by the wall,   32
When I was sick and lay a-bed,   95
Whether the weather be fine   15
Who would true valour see,   94
Why, who makes much of a miracle?   88

Under the greenwood tree   96